Original title:
The Brooch of Beauty

Copyright © 2025 Creative Arts Management OÜ
All rights reserved.

Author: Milo Harrington
ISBN HARDBACK: 978-1-80586-215-4
ISBN PAPERBACK: 978-1-80586-687-9

Traces of Elegance

There once was a gem on a bright display,
Residing on jackets, it danced and swayed.
With laughter it sparkled, a glimmering friend,
Telling the tales of the style we defend.

A pin shaped like a cat, what a curious sight,
It winked at the world, oh what pure delight!
Said, 'Never mind trends, let your spirit be grand,'
As it jiggled and jangled while taking a stand.

In gardens of fashion where colors bloom bright,
It prances and twirls in the soft morning light.
Adorning old sweaters that seem quite forlorn,
It gives them new life, like a gown newly worn.

So if you feel drab and your outfit seems flat,
Just find a fine piece, or a silly old hat!
With sparkles and giggles, our hearts it will seize,
Traces of elegance, wear it with ease.

Aria of Adornment

A pin like a bird on a summer's day,
Sang sweet little tunes in a curious way.
It perched on a collar, and then it took flight,
Leaving behind laughter that soared through the night.

With colors so vivid, it shocked even cats,
Fashioned from glitter and old fancy bats.
It twirled on a dress, causing giggles to flow,
An aria echoing 'Yes! Let's steal the show!'

Oh, how it would tease and beguile each glance,
No need for a mirror, let whimsy enhance!
The life of the party with jokes on the side,
Adorned in such charm, oh where could it hide?

So join in the fun, slip on that bright flair,
And see how the world will turn with a stare.
The layers of laughter, the joy we surround,
In an aria of adornment, we twirl all around.

Ethereal Glimmers

A sparkling gem on a cat's fine ear,
Winks and twirls, spreading good cheer.
It whispers tales of a dazzling night,
Where socks and shoes got into a fight.

Laughter dances in the air so bright,
As it giggles softly, what a delight!
In a world of tedium, it vows to ignite,
A chuckle, a scoff, heart's true height.

Infinite Gleam

A shiny trinket on a squirrel's tail,
Wobbling around, oh what a tale!
With each little twist and every shake,
It tickles the trees, for goodness' sake.

The moon takes notice, with a smirk so sly,
A wink for the stars, a wink for the sky.
The world is absurd, yet we carry on,
Chasing the glimmers from dusk till dawn.

A Shimmering Journey

In Grandma's drawer, what a find so rare,
A quirky pin that makes everyone stare.
With jellybeans stuck like jewels in its frame,
It sparkles and giggles, calling your name.

Worn on a blouse, it busts out in flair,
Confetti and laughter float everywhere.
No occasion too silly, no moment too meek,
It drags out the merry, it's truly unique.

The Cultured Mark

A dazzling patch on a penguin's hat,
Puffs up with pride, oh what's up with that?
It challenges norms, fashion's old scheme,
With a wink and a nod, it dares you to dream.

In a world of drab, it struts with style,
Making owls swoon and hedgehogs smile.
Artistic, bizarre, what a visual treat,
Spinning tall tales under its funky beat.

Elegance Embodied

A shimmering clasp on a dog's fur,
It sways like a dance, oh what a stir!
A very fine jewel on a pizza slice,
The world finds it odd, but ah, how nice!

When worn by a cat on a wild afternoon,
It sparkles and winks like a cheeky moon.
Cats strut with confidence, hearts so light,
With gems on their tails, it's a laughable sight!

Captivating Glint

A duo of socks, mismatched and bright,
With a shimmer of sparkle, they're quite a sight.
They catch everyone's eye, a glorious mess,
Fashion faux pas? No way, it's a success!

A lad with a wink and a flowered hat,
Struts down the street, and oh, fancy that!
With a twinkle of flair in his pocket he brings,
The laughter erupts, oh, how joyfully sings!

Hidden Charms

Tucked in the fur of an old grandma's coat,
A secret of laughter, oh, who would've wrote?
Beneath layers of history, a flower so sweet,
With soft giggles hidden, it's quite the treat!

Longing gazes at brownies, oh what a sight,
With sprinkles and sparkles that make taste buds ignite!
Each slice carries tales of delectable charm,
With every bite taken, it lifts any qualm!

Kaleidoscope of Finery

In the circus of life, imagine the fun,
A unicycle juggler sparkles under the sun.
With polka dots dancing like popcorn in air,
His outfit's so bold, it's beyond compare!

Glittering marbles, they tumble and spin,
Like a carousel of whimsy, just let the fun in.
With colors so wild, they play hide and seek,
Turning smiles up wide, it's cheeky and sleek!

The Allure of Gems

A shiny pebble caught my eye,
I thought it grand, a wink might fly.
In pockets deep, it made its bed,
A sparkler left, my wallet bled.

"With sparkles bright, I'll fool the crew!"
They gasped, they laughed, they knew it too.
"I'm rich!" I claimed, with flair so bold,
But stuck at home, my gems are sold.

Enchanted Trinkets

A necklace tossed upon the floor,
Would my cat wear it? What a bore!
She pranced about, all regal, grand,
While I just watched, a goldfish bland.

Each bracelet whispers tales of yore,
A story, yes, but who keeps score?
I wore it out, but hey, oh dear!
The clasp then popped, oh not my gear!

Reflections of Allure

In mirrors bright, I strike a pose,
With gems afire, like a rose.
But selfies seemed to catch my chin,
Why do I wear this blingy spin?

With every flick, I lose my charm,
Who thought a spark would cause such harm?
A shiny lure, all eyes will gawk,
Yet clumsy me, I trip and talk.

Splendid Secrets

A simple plan to dazzle friends,
With glimmering stones, the laughter blends.
But as I strut, a tear appears,
Turns out my gem's just made of cheers!

An opal found in grandma's drawer,
"Is it real?" I asked with lore.
"Dear child," she said, "it's all pretend,
But laughter's what you really spend!"

Celestial Embellishments

Stars from space, they twinkle bright,
I wore one once, it gave a fright!
A comet slipped right off my dress,
I tripped and fell, oh what a mess!

With moons that glow and suns that shine,
They say I'm chic, I think they're fine.
But when the wind begins to puff,
My sparkly gems just aren't enough!

Jewels of Dream

Dreams I wear like crowns on sleep,
They sparkle, twinkle, never beep.
Last night a gem started to hum,
I thought it was my friend's old drum!

I danced around with pearls so bright,
But lost my shoe, oh what a sight!
With diamonds laughing in the sun,
My fashion sense? Oh, just for fun!

Enchanted Embellishment

Once I wore a charm of glee,
It wiggled, jiggled, full of spree.
A pixie gave it just for laughs,
Now it's my dog's favorite path!

When I step out, it starts to sing,
Neighbors think I've lost my bling.
With sparkles, sparkles, all around,
Who says fashion can't be found?

The Locket's Secret

Locked within a heart-shaped frame,
A mystery, oh what a game!
Each time I peek, I see a sock,
I think my locket must have rock!

My friends all giggle, calling me,
"Fashion fool, can't you see?"
Yet still I wear it, proud and bold,
A story wrapped in threads of gold!

Glimmers of Elegance

A shiny pin on a coat, so grand,
It dazzles folks across the land.
But when it slips and makes a dive,
The dog now wears it, oh what a jive!

With sparkles that catch the eye so sly,
It winks and nods, oh how we sigh.
Yet under the couch it found a home,
In the land of lost socks, it loves to roam.

Fabulous flair, with tales to tell,
From fashionista to a cat, oh well!
Fate's fickle grace, a twist of fate,
Who knew a pin could juggle so great?

In memories cherished, with laughter shared,
Each shining moment, slightly impaired.
Through mishaps and giggles, it weaves its spell,
A whimsical charm, we know it well.

Jewel of Enchantment

In twilight whispers, a spark does gleam,
A quirky gem from a wild dream.
Stuck on a hat that flies away,
Chasing it down? Oh, what a ballet!

With a wink, it shows its playful side,
It flirts with hats and takes a ride.
But oh, it's lost in a scoop of ice,
The sweetest of treats, not so nice!

Sparkling with laughter, a jester's laugh,
This jewel's antics make the world daft.
With each tiny prance, it finds its muse,
A merry little dance, too fun to lose.

In the clutches of grace, all joking aside,
This gem's not just pretty, it'll ride the tide.
Through mishap and mirth, it shines ever bright,
A treasure of humor, quite the delight.

Whispered Adornments

A twinkle here, a shimmer there,
"Is that a bug?" folks often stare.
But wait! It's just the bling on me,
A glorious dance of absurdity!

Once pinned on the cat, it nearly flew,
A pirate treasure in a tale so blue.
With giggles erupting, minds running wild,
This charm's sense of humor never reviled.

It whispers softly, "Look at me sway,"
A rogue, a jester, come out to play.
With every bounce, it sings a tune,
Lifting spirits high like a cartoon balloon.

So if you spot it, give a cheer,
For adornments like these are full of cheer.
In a world of serious spins and frowns,
Find joy in the absurd, where laughter abounds.

Shimmering Essence

A piece of flair on a common shirt,
Transforming the dull into quirk and flirt.
Every glance meets a giggle or chortle,
As it glimmers bright, what a marvel!

With each jangling laugh, it tells a tale,
Of a wobbly journey on a giant snail.
"Look at me now!" it giggles with glee,
An unlikely hero, oh can't you see?

It wanders free, never to stay,
From pockets to plates, it makes its way.
Through puddles and rain, a wily sprite,
Finding joy in chaos, such a delight!

So here's to the sparkles, the laughter they bring,
A hint of the silly in everything.
With each swift twirl, it hints and it jests,
Immortalized moments, in giggles, we rest.

Shimmering Whispers

A sparkly gem took flight,
Danced around the room all night.
It said, "I'm more than just a stance,
Join me in this silly dance!"

With a wink and gleam so bright,
It twirled under the moonlight.
But tripped on its own glitzy flair,
And landed in a furry chair!

A cat with style took the scoop,
Now that's a dazzling group!
With laughter echoing so clear,
They posed for selfies—oh dear, oh dear!

So if you find a shiny gem,
Just know it has a wildhem.
It might just make you laugh anew,
Life's better with a silly hue!

Enchanted Adornments

In a land where jewels giggle,
The diamonds started to wiggle.
They threw a party, what a sight,
With glitter balls and sparkles bright!

A ruby played on a funky flute,
While sapphires danced in silly boots.
The pearl jumped high, then made a splash,
While opals laughed and made a crash!

The emeralds rolled on the floor,
As amethyst asked for more encore.
With every twirl and silly prank,
The audience rose to give a rank!

So if you hear a sparkle's cheer,
Join the fun—don't you fear!
For in this world of shiny glee,
Adornments bring us pure esprit!

Radiance Unveiled

A glittery star, oh what a tease,
It blinked at folks like a mischievous breeze.
"Come closer," it winked with flair,
To have a laugh, if you dare!"

Behind the curtain, a shimmered prank,
Jewels dressed in colors rank.
They played a game of fashion fights,
Wearing socks with sparkling tights!

Each gem decided it was time,
For a comedy gala, oh so prime.
With jokes that sparkled, puns that shined,
Even the dullest joined and dined!

So let your jewels giggle and gleam,
For laughter sparkles like a dream.
Wear a smile, it's the best adrift,
In this radiant, silly gift!

Delicate Treasures

A tiny treasure in a box,
Whispered secrets, just like fox.
"Hey, I'm not just pretty face,
I've got some moves, watch my grace!"

It skipped and hopped, oh what fun,
Outshining every moonlit run.
"I'll charm you with my glitter flair,
Now, will you dare to take this dare?"

Each twinkle told a cheeky joke,
And made the other trinkets poke.
"With a giggle and a shimmy too,
Who knew this shine would steal the view?"

So if you see a twinkling glance,
Join the fun—come take a chance!
For even treasures, old or new,
Love a laugh; it's true, it's true!

Serene Splendor

In a world of glitz and glow,
A lady danced, with moves so slow.
Her sparkly gem, it twinkled wide,
But it fell off and took a ride.

The cat thought it was a toy,
He batted it with feline joy.
It rolled away, cause quite a fuss,
As everyone screamed, "What's the fuss?"

The gem then rolled into a pie,
The baker yelled, "Oh no, oh my!"
Now crusty treats in a sparkly mess,
Everyone laughed, what a wild dress!

Next morning came a fancy feast,
With jewel-encrusted donuts at least.
It sparkled bright within the glaze,
The guests all cheered, "What a craze!"

Infusion of Glam

A dainty lady dressed so spry,
Sipped her tea and let out a sigh.
Her hat adorned with feathers grand,
But oh my, it started to stand!

It flopped and flailed, like a bird at sea,
Knocking over her cup of tea.
The guests erupted, laughter loud,
'This party surely isn't proud!'

She gathered her hat, with elegance rare,
But girl, that wind just didn't care!
It danced away, on a whimsy path,
Leaving her wondering, "What's the math?"

With every flap, the hat took flight,
Bumping into all within sight.
Each twirl and swirl was pure delight,
Who knew glam could cause such fright?

Radiant Essence

A shiny gem upon my chest,
Glimmers bright, I feel so blessed.
But wait, what's that? A bit of drool,
From my pup, who thinks it's a jewel!

He leaps and bounds, a playful thief,
Chasing sparkles, adding to the grief.
I shout, "No, don't eat that shiny thing!"
But he's busy howling, oh what a fling!

It landed softly in the soup,
Oh dear, now we've a sparkly scoop!
The guests all stared, eyes open wide,
"Is this a dish for fancy pride?"

With spoons held high, they took a taste,
"Is it magic or just a waste?"
Laughter filled the room, oh how they'd rave,
From a little gem, they found their wave!

The Dream of Delicacy

A dainty dance upon the floor,
With butterflies and gems galore.
But as she twirls, her shoe flew high,
It hit the wall, oh my oh my!

The guests all stared, with eyes aflame,
"For such a dance, it's quite a game!"
The host was served, a shoe surprise,
They laughed so hard, it lit the skies!

Onlookers placed bets on shoes,
Each foot adorned with eccentric hues.
One lady lost hers in a swirl,
It turned into a shoe parade, oh girl!

Now every step, a curious plight,
Sparkles and giggles filled the night.
They danced and laughed under the stars,
In shoes that dazzled, we're all bizarre!

Woven Whispers

In a realm where odd things dwell,
A pin that giggles like a bell.
It compliments my mismatched shoes,
Whispering secrets, oh what a muse!

With sparkles tied to a polka-dot,
Hiccups from laughter are all I've got.
The cat tries to swipe it away,
While I prance like it's my birthday!

Each time I wear it, I get a grin,
Even the mirror can't hold it in.
Reflecting smiles, it winks, oh dear!
Making daily life such good cheer!

So here's to the joy that it brings near,
With every old joke, and silly cheer.
For in each pin, a tale takes flight,
A shimmering spark in the day and night.

A Dance of Light

When I prance in my sparkle attire,
People laugh at my sparkly higher.
It twists and twirls with a life of its own,
Sometimes it dances like a live drone!

At every party, it steals the show,
Guiding my steps with a glimmering glow.
"Is it jewelry or a firefly?" they jest,
As I zip past, bringing out the best!

With a jig and a twist, I swirl around,
My shiny companion, it never backs down.
It's not just a clasp, it's a spectacle wide,
A true dance partner, all day by my side!

So let's cheer to the glow and the gleam,
This dazzling friend of mine makes me beam.
It's not quiet; it sings like a breeze,
In its shimmer, I find joy with ease.

Adorned Elegance

With class and style, it sits on my vest,
A delicate charm that never takes rest.
It winks at the folks who later remark,
"Is it fashion or folly? Let's throw a spark!"

I wore it to dinner, it stole the bread,
Looking all fancy, it still made me dread.
For every bite taken, it gleamed with glee,
Saying, "Oh darling, look at me!"

Friends chuckle as I try to be chic,
While it plots to draw all the attention, so sleek.
"Did your brooch get into mischief again?"
"Did it trip the waiter or dance with his pen?"

As we laugh over drinks and silly lore,
My elegant pin only craves for more.
In the end, it's not just a look—but fun,
A playful spark, just weighing a ton!

Gems of Grace

Oh, these gems of humor, they dance on my thread,
Winking, they gossip with joy instead.
A sapphire wink, a ruby chuckle,
Who knew elegance could cause such a buckle?

As I strut with my radiant flair,
They're saying, "Oh honey, don't you dare!
To trip in laughter would be a delight,
Let's sprinkle giggles in the shimmering light."

At every corner, a jest is laid,
These gems at play, they're never delayed.
A clink, a clank, and suddenly, behold,
Everyone's joined in, their stories unfold!

So, let's toast to the moments we share,
With gems of grace dancing everywhere.
For beauty isn't just in how we present,
But in laughter shared, with joy content!

Elegance in Motion

A jewel that dances with a laugh,
It twinkles brightly, what a gaffe.
On my lapel, it takes center stage,
Like a peacock strutting, it's all the rage.

It wiggles and jigs, oh what a sight,
Glimmers of glam in morning light.
Friends tease me, 'What flair you possess!'
I simply grin, 'It's my happy dress!'

I wore it once at a fancy soirée,
The cat showed up, in disarray.
It mistook my gem for a shiny toy,
Chased it around, oh what a ploy!

Now every event feels like a show,
With giggles and glances, it steals the glow.
A charm of chuckles as I strut,
Rolling with grace, not just a nut!

A Token of Refinement

A little charm that knows its worth,
Turns heads and causes quite a mirth.
On a dull evening, it's quite the blast,
With a cheeky wink, it makes fun last.

Friends gather round with a look of glee,
'What on earth is that? Is it fancy tea?'
I chuckle back, 'It's not for sips,
But for showing off my fashion flips!'

It's not just metal, it's a big quirk,
Dances in light with a silly smirk.
At times it trips, oh what a mess,
I laugh and say, 'It's just a dress!'

In crowded cafes, it steals the show,
Like a puppy that's ready to go.
With jests and japes, it jingles bright,
A token of joy by day and night!

The Alluring Trinket

A sparkly doodad, not very shy,
It winks and giggles, oh my oh my!
Hanging on my coat, it prances free,
Like it knows all the gossip, believe you me.

At parties it steals, not just the cake,
Witty remarks, it loves to make.
'I see you've brought your shiny guide,'
One friend remarks, eyes opened wide.

If only it could chat and boast,
It would share tales of my fondest toast.
With friends around, it spins in delight,
Echoing laughter that lasts through the night.

But mind you, it's rather vain,
Can't stand to be near a full-length pane.
With a twist and a turn, it sways away,
Chasing shadows, come what may!

Harmony of Design

A little sparkle with a touch of fun,
Oh what a show, it steals the run!
Mounted on fabric, a flashy sight,
Who needs a spotlight? I've got this light!

With giggles and twists, it makes me dance,
Beneath the moonlight, it takes a chance.
'Where'd you get that?' my best friend sighs,
'At the junk shop, with the funny pies!'

It jests with flair, it's questionably proud,
Makes crowd members laugh, cheers out loud.
Wherever I go, it tags along,
Dancing with humor, oh what a throng!

So here's to the glimmer that brings a grin,
Joy wrapped in an oval, where laughs begin.
In a world so serious, let's share a jest,
With elegance and giggles, life feels blessed!

Glimmering Secrets

In a world where sparkles dance,
A clumsy cat took quite a chance,
With jeweled tail and winking eye,
She caught a glimmer flashing by.

A tiny gem that rolled away,
She chased it all through bright of day,
But every pounce and leap she'd make,
Ended with a little quake.

Her friends all giggled, tails a-swish,
As she would leap and then would wish,
For grace that seemed beyond her reach,
The chase was quite a funny speech.

In the end, the gem was found,
On her nose, it gleamed around,
With every step, a stumble shy,
That silly cat just couldn't fly.

A Pin of Perfection

A simple pin upon my coat,
Declared itself a grand devote,
It anchored notes and crumbs so well,
Yet often held a secret spell.

When guests would come and hats would sway,
It'd wink, distract, and lead astray,
With every lost and found delight,
A pin that sparkled into night.

It shot confetti in a whirl,
As if to tease the dancing girl,
And shyly laughed when feathers flew,
Because it knew just what to do.

Oh, what a joy to wear that pin,
A masterpiece of subtle sin,
For every hug might take a chance,
To launch the laughter and the dance.

Luminous Allure

A twinkling piece sat on the shelf,
Spouted tales of past itself,
With every flash, it told a joke,
To have it on, oh what a poke!

It slipped and slid, a daring feat,
Made even the shyest dancers meet,
"Not on my dress!" a lady cried,
As it rolled off with gleeful pride.

It knew its charm, it wore a grin,
As mismatched socks began to spin,
With laughter loud and clinking cups,
The allure brought out all the pups.

So raise a glass, give it a cheer,
For every laugh, it draws you near,
A shimmer of laughter in the room,
With every sparkle, we'd laugh and bloom.

The Pendant's Tale

There once was a pendant on a chain,
That claimed to ease all kinds of pain,
With every jingle, it would sway,
A reminder that life's a play.

It told of clumsy steps and falls,
Of nights spent answering the calls,
Of fashion trials and funny sights,
Adorning everyone in sparkly lights.

But one day it went for a swim,
And from that day, things got a bit grim,
It bubbled up with frothy glee,
A pendant lost in the big blue sea!

Yet still it sparkled on the sand,
With boasts of parties, oh so grand,
Though tides may come and waves may crash,
The laughter from it will always last.

Radiance Captured

A glint that twinkles on my lapel,
I pin it on, oh what the hell!
It sparkles bright, a tiny light,
The talk of town, oh what a sight!

My cat walks by, gives it a stare,
As if it's saying, 'Do I dare?'
I laugh aloud, it's just a game,
This gem of mine, it brings me fame!

Friends all gather, asking, 'Where?'
Just on my chest, it's quite a flair!
They compliment, they giggle too,
For who knew jewels could be so blue?

With every move, it dances there,
Reflecting dreams, igniting flair.
In all its glory, full of cheer,
My tiny gem, I hold it dear!

Embers of Grace

A little spark, it winks and grins,
On my jacket, where fun begins.
It glows all night, a cheeky tease,
As I trip over my own unease!

It shakes and shimmies when I dance,
To make it shine, I take the chance.
Friends laugh loud, they dance around,
My tiny star, it won't fall down!

It clashes bright with my flour sack,
But I don't care, I need no flak.
With every twirl, it steals a glance,
This silly jewel, oh how it prance!

Through dinners served and drinks all spilled,
My sparkly friend just won't be stilled.
It says, "Let's laugh, let's live this night!"
With twinkling joy, it feels just right!

The Charm Within

A little shiny, quite profound,
On my coat, it's often found.
Its gleam attracts the oddest stares,
A conversation starter, it declares!

With every move, it shows some sass,
While I just worry—will I pass?
But look at that, it steals the show,
My quirky gem, the world should know!

'Is it a star?' my neighbor quips,
Or merely nice, on fashion tips?
I shrug and smile; what do I care?
Just look at how it shines with flair!

It twirls around, a playful sprite,
Daring anyone to join the fight.
With humor bold and heart so true,
This charming piece has much to do!

Splendor in Stillness

In quiet moments, it gleams and shows,
On a simple shirt, it brightly glows.
A little charm, oh what a flair,
Who knew fab could just be there?

Friends are here, they point, they jest,
'Look at that gem, it's truly blessed!'
I simply smile, enjoying the jest,
As laughter swirls, this is the best!

But when I sit to sip my tea,
It catches light, and oh, so free!
A moment's grace, it takes the prize,
Winking back with sparkling eyes!

So bring your style, your charm, your cheer,
With giggles shared, let's all draw near.
For in this fun, we find our bliss,
And celebrate that cheeky kiss!

Infinitesimal Elegance

In the corner sat a tiny gem,
It sparkled like a cheeky phlegm.
A dance party for ants, no less,
Wearing it causes pure distress.

It swayed on a dainty pin,
With all the charm of a paper bin.
Bumblebees tried to steal the show,
But it laughed and said, 'Oh no, no, no!'

It caught the eye of a clumsy squirrel,
Who wore it like a bright pink whirl.
Dancing rounds with sparkling flair,
Leaving all other nuts in despair.

Oh what joy in a gleaming speck,
That could cause such a fashion wreck!
With laughter echoing far and wide,
In the land where style is the best ride.

Crafting of Glamour

In a workshop dusty, slightly grim,
Lies a treasure with an odd whim.
Made of buttons and mismatched lace,
Worn on coats, it puts smiles on face.

A feather here, a googly eye,
A jewel that makes owls go 'Oh my!'
Crafted with care, yet riddled with jest,
It outshines the fanciest of the best.

The artist grins, brush in hand,
Wonders aloud, 'Is this what they planned?'
With glue and glitter, a masterpiece born,
Prompting laughter until the dawn.

Oh, the beauty of what we create,
With a wink, a giggle, and maybe some fate.
In this realm of jests and glee,
True glamour is more than we can see.

The Jewel's Legacy

Once a diamond from a cheery stream,
Turned into a coward's dream.
It lost a battle with a cookie crumb,
And now just hides, feeling so glum.

An heirloom passed from hand to hand,
Goes to a family far too bland.
It rolls away on a rainy day,
Screaming, 'Why can't I have a say?'

Adventurous life, oh how it seemed,
But it never got to be the gleamed.
Instead, it became the family dog's toy,
A legacy that brings both pain and joy.

Though trapped in chaos, it wears a crown,
Amongst the ruckus, a jewel renowned.
Its twinkle shines bright in laughter's wake,
Leaving all pretensions in its wake.

A Touch of Opulence

Amidst the clutter of sparkly things,
Lurks a find that laughter brings.
A button that thinks it's a royal decree,
Proclaiming its riches with utmost glee.

It fell from grace, or so it's said,
Mocking all who claimed it's dead.
On a hat, it gives the best flair,
While birds whisper, 'What a wacky pair!'

Oh how it glimmers, and shines so bright,
Demanding attention, a comical sight.
Its opulence is found in each little fail,
A crown of charm in this playful tale.

When laughter echoes in style's embrace,
This flamboyant piece takes its place.
In a world of fashion, it makes its stand,
With humor and grace, a sparkling brand.

Threads of Timelessness

In the attic, I found some lace,
Long forgotten, but full of grace.
My cat wore it, looked quite grand,
A royal meow, a noble stand.

Spools of colors, tangled mess,
My sewing skills, I must confess.
A shirt I made, oh what a sight,
My friend laughed, I took a flight.

With each thread, a story spun,
Of stylish fails and endless fun.
I wear my flaws like a crown,
In fashion's game, I'll never frown.

So here's to threads, and laughs galore,
In this wardrobe, who could ask for more?
For in each stitch, hilarity flows,
As I don my cape, everyone knows!

Consumed by Beauty

Once I tried a fancy hat,
Became a pigeon's favorite spat.
Strutting 'round with flair and glee,
Until it turned to lunch, oh me!

Lipstick dreams and blushing skin,
I swiped it on with wild spin.
A clownish face in vibrant hue,
My date just laughed, oh what to do?

Mirrors crack with each new style,
My fashion sense? Purely versatile.
Each accessory a battle won,
But oh, the mirror's not that fun!

Consumed by looks, I take a bow,
But who needs beauty, anyhow?
With a wink and jest, I stride away,
In my own quirky, lovely way!

The Art of Adornments

A necklace made from soda caps,
Worn to dinner, raised a few claps.
"Is that vintage?" friends would muse,
As I nodded, trying to refuse.

Earrings crafted from old spoons,
Twinkling bright under silly moons.
I jangled them with every step,
Waltzing like a clumsy rep!

An oversized brooch of cheese,
Fashion statements that aim to please.
"Delicious!" said my hungry friend,
When I wear it, no need to blend.

In artful chaos, I find my flair,
Adornments spark joy, beyond compare.
So let the world giggle and tease,
For I wear my quirks with such ease!

Whimsy in Elegance

At tea, I wore a dress of rags,
With mismatched socks and tote of bags.
My friends raised brows, then bursts of cheer,
Elegance? Sport it, oh dear!

Glitter glue and funky hats,
Who needs pearls when you've got spats?
With every sip, a challenge declared,
Frog-themed cups and pastries shared!

Twirling twirls in my polka dots,
Confidence growing in crazy spots.
No rules here, just laughter and grace,
As elegance joins in the race.

So here's to whimsy, loud and bold,
In a world where stories unfold.
Let's dress for joy, not for the show,
And dance like no one—now that's the glow!

Radiant Whimsy

In a land where odd things dance with glee,
A squirrel wears pearls, feel the jubilee!
A cat in a hat struts like a queen,
While the goldfish issues beauty regime.

An octopus spins, with a glittery tail,
Whirling confetti, it leaves quite the trail!
The hedgehog applies a fine shade of pink,
While penguins sip tea, giving winks.

Daisies now sport a flamboyant bow,
As bumblebees gossip, they steal the show!
The moon smirks down, it's all in good fun,
A carnival of quirks has just begun!

So join in the laughter, wear something absurd,
Let that whimsical spirit go unheard!
With creatures so charming, bizarre and bright,
Life's little jewels are pure delight!

Sparkling Recollections

Once a penguin lost his favorite tie,
While waltzing with donuts beneath the sky,
A parrot squawks, "You're a sight to behold!"
With shades and a bow, so outrageously bold!

In the attic of laughs, we find treasures deep,
A unicorn juggles while monkeys leap,
Each quirk in the box tells a wild tale,
Of mishaps and giggles that never go stale!

So grab a fond memory and put on a hat,
Dance with the stories, imagine that!
Laughter erupts with each sparkling glance,
As elephants waltz in a one-legged dance!

And when we look back, with smiles on our face,
Each silly adventure finds its perfect place,
With memories so bright, they twinkle and shine,
The funniest moments are truly divine!

Enchanted Reflections

A mirror that giggles, what could this mean?
It shows silly faces, a true comic scene!
A frog sings opera, it thinks it's quite grand,
While fairies throw marshmallows with their tiny hands.

A puppy in pearls leads a parade,
As cats with top hats perform a charade,
The moonlight is tickled, it starts to dance,
While raccoons wear skirts, hopping at chance!

With laughter like bubbles, they float in the air,
Filled with sparkles that twirl everywhere,
They roll on the ground, all covered in glee,
In a realm where enchantment is wild and free!

So cherish the moments, let whimsy take flight,
For laughter's the magic that lights up the night,
In this land of reflections, so charmingly spun,
We find all the beauty is simply pure fun!

Celestial Charms

Aliens visit with dance moves so bright,
They twirl through the stars, it's a cosmic delight!
With tinfoil hats and shoes made of cheese,
They giggle and topple, just aiming to please.

A comet sells tickets to a lunar show,
Where planets sing jingles, putting on a glow,
Space kittens chase comets, in zero-G flight,
While shooting stars sparkle, igniting the night!

Candidates of charm take the stage to prance,
Each one more quirky than the last in this dance,
Galactic laughter resonates far and wide,
As they shimmy with glee, nothing left to hide.

So orbit around laughter, let it unfurl,
In a universe painted in shades of pure swirl,
For all cosmic treasures, we'll celebrate cheer,
In this realm of charm, joy's always near!

Gilded Mystique

In a drawer of glitter and sheen,
Lies a treasure fit for a queen.
It sparkles and winks with a grin,
I'd wear it, but can't find my chin!

A clasp that's twisted, a pin so thin,
A battle of fashion, my head's in a spin.
With every twist, a laugh does ensue,
What a scene when I finally break through!

The gem is so grand, it rivals the sun,
But where goes the sparkle when I start to run?
Chasing my cat while trying to look slick
He pounced for my ear—yikes! What a trick!

So here I stand, with hair askew,
My outfit's a jigsaw, and oh, how I flew!
Yet in this madcap, I can't help but cheer,
For even in chaos, my style is quite clear!

Fusion of Radiance

At the county fair, I took a bold chance,
To pin on my charm with a whimsical dance.
But chicken on a stick was my real delight,
My accessory rolled away, oh what a sight!

A glimmering circle was lost in the grass,
My game of tag turned into a farce.
With a dash for my bling, I tripped on a chair,
As the crowd roared with laughter, I knew I was rare.

I found it at last, in a clown's big shoe,
He chuckled and winked, "This belongs to you!"
Worn on my jacket, it shone like a star,
Though the grease on my fingers made it raise an eyebrow.

Now every event, I'm ready to show,
With laughter and flair, I steal the whole show.
So here's to that charm, with its silly tale,
A fusion of chaos that'll always prevail!

Celestial Adornment

In a sky of sequins, I plan to ascend,
With jewels like comets, my fashion will blend.
But trying to shine like the night sky up high,
I bumped into Mars—oh, my oh my!

With silver and gold in a cosmic swirl,
I dabble with style like a space-bound girl.
Yet planets they giggle when I trip on the moon,
As stardust showers down, I just laugh too soon.

Galaxy gems that whisper and twirl,
Look out, here comes another wardrobe whirl!
My rocket's a wreck, oh, what did I wear?
The stars twinkle brightly at my fashion despair.

In this universe wild, I wear it with pride,
With each cosmic misstep, my humor won't hide.
For shining so bright in a slinky space fog,
Who knew being fabulous could feel like a slog?

Lacy Echoes

With ribbons and lace, I dress to impress,
But tangled I get, oh dear what a mess!
As I fumble and fidget like a puppet on string,
My friends all collapse, what laughter they bring!

An echo of glamour that twirls in my hand,
Yet caught on my sleeve, it's a sight so unplanned.
With every tug, another snare I find,
My outfit's a riddle, a real fashion bind.

In a game of peekaboo with my own self,
I trip on my lace, and off goes the shelf!
With a flourish I tumble, a dance made for fame,
"Oh darling, you shine!" they shout out my name!

So I rise from the chaos, my grin shining bright,
With laughter and lace, I wield my delight.
For life's just a loop, where we twirl and we sway,
In the echo of joy, I find my own way!

Mystique of Embellishment

A sparkly gem upon my chest,
It dances wild, it wears a jest.
My friends all ask, 'What's that you flaunt?'
I say, 'Just magic, it's a real haunt!'

In every light, it winks and smiles,
A treasure found in quirky styles.
It giggles softly, takes a bow,
And makes my plainest shirt wow now!

With every glance, it's quite the tease,
It juggles colors like a breeze.
I swear it whispers silly jokes,
Like a tiny gem that provokes!

So wear your sparkles without restraint,
Let everything be what it ain't.
For in this world, we're gems and more,
Laughing as we dance, that's the core!

Luminous Echoes

My badge of honor, shining bright,
It steals the show, it's quite the sight.
With every twinkle, it starts to sing,
A chorus of laughs, a merry ring!

It bounces light like crazy bugs,
It says, 'Wear me, forget the shrugs!'
Each shimmer tells a silly tale,
Of silly dances and crazy hail.

Adventures grand, with me in tow,
A crystal friend, we steal the show.
Together we'll cause a playful stir,
As I spin around, my style's a blur!

So grab your sparkles, don't be shy,
Let them twirl and fly so high!
With joy and laughter, we'll explore,
With flashes of fun, who could want more?

Refined Radiance

Dressed in glimmer, a sight to see,
With laughter echoing, just like me.
With a wink and nod, it takes the stage,
A dazzling friend, uncaged from a cage!

Join the party, don't be late,
A whispered secret, a chuckle bait.
It spins in circles, a jester bold,
With secrets more than jewels of gold.

I laugh along as it starts to glow,
This cheeky charm steals every show.
Together we shimmy like the best of mates,
In this wild dance, all doubts abate!

Let's sparkle more, let's shine so bright,
With a flick of joy, we own the night!
Exploring gleeful paths to tread,
With every giggle, a spark is fed!

Charmed Journey

On an adventure with my shiny gem,
Each step we take, a diadem.
It laughs aloud at grumpy frowns,
A cheeky glint that flips around!

It rolls and twirls like a roller skate,
Winks at the world, never late!
'Pick me up!' it shouts with glee,
'In every moment, let's be free!'

With swirls of color, it leads the way,
Joking through night and every day.
In this wild waltz of silly delight,
We sparkle bright, a sheer delight!

So join me now, let's never part,
With mischief stitched within our heart.
For on this journey, we shall roam,
With laughter loud, we've found our home!

Dazzling Sentiments

A shiny pin on my attire,
It catches eyes, never tires.
With every glance, a chuckle found,
As I strut about, all around.

It sparkles bright, like stars at night,
A tiny gem that feels just right.
It jabs my shirt, a playful twist,
Who knew fashion could be such bliss?

My friends all stare, then burst with glee,
This comedy on me, they see.
With every laugh, I twirl and bow,
This lovely trinket steals the show.

So here I stand, with joy so true,
A shiny piece that makes me blue.
But wait, I mean, it makes me bright,
Oh what a sight, oh what a night!

A Spark of Enchantment

In sunshine's gleam, it winks at me,
A glimmering piece of fancy spree.
With sparkly laughs that dance and play,
It charms the dullest, brightens the gray.

I wore it once on laundry day,
It matched the soap, oh what a fray!
The dryer banged and spun about,
My fashion sense, a laughing shout.

Each twinkle brings a funny tale,
Of mishaps, slips, and goofy fails.
Yet through the chaos, smiles arise,
For laughter is a sweet surprise.

So here I twirl, a spark divine,
My little gem, a friend of mine.
It whispers jokes that never end,
The best of gifts, a trusty friend!

Charmed by Delicacy

A dainty piece upon my dress,
With colors bright, it can impress.
But as I move, it takes a dive,
Oh no, it slipped, is it alive?

I chase it down, it rolls away,
Like a small cat that loves to play.
With friends I laugh, and so do they,
"Your fashion sense is quite the ballet!"

They say it's art, this lovely thing,
But all I feel is a pinball fling.
A charm so sweet, it leads the dance,
Yet sometimes trips me in my pants!

So here we are, a charming scene,
A delicate laugh, a fashion queen.
With every twirl, I face my fate,
At least I'm clad in something great!

Threads of Gleam

A clutch of gems, a twinkling thread,
Caressing laughter as it spreads.
With every wink, I feel so grand,
A jester's crown, a playful stand.

I wear it well, or so I think,
But sideways glances make me wink.
"Oh look!" they say, "What a show!"
As I fumble, graceful like a crow.

Through every slip and every grin,
This gleaming piece wears quite a spin.
It dances 'round, and so do I,
In threads of mirth, we fly so high.

So here I shine, a shining dream,
A little spark of laugh and gleam.
With friends who cheer and love to tease,
This joyful ride is sure to please!

Essence of Luxury

In a box, you thought so grand,
A shiny pin, across your hand.
You wore it bold, with all your might,
But it turned your blouse to fright!

It sparkled bright, like disco ball,
Danced around at the gala hall.
Yet when you sat, it made a noise,
Like a cat being chased by boys!

Your cousin laughed, she couldn't cease,
Said, "That's fashion with a piece!"
You smiled wide, a laugh in store,
And swore you'd wear it nevermore!

But deep down, the love still gleamed,
A funny story, as it seemed.
You cherish that peculiar flair,
A luxury to laugh and share!

The Gemstone Diary

In a tiny case, there lay a gem,
You thought it fine, a true diadem.
You wore it once, oh what a sight,
But it rolled away, oh what a fright!

A game of fetch with the dog at play,
Chasing sparkles all the way.
It landed, plop, in the fishy tank,
What a catch! Oh, what a prank!

Your fish adorned with bling so bright,
Swam like stars in the moonlit night.
With laughter loud, you took a snap,
A furry friend, the fish had blap!

Now in the scrapbook, tales reside,
Of gems that swim and dogs that slide.
Who knew such fun could be a vice,
In a vibrant world, we paid the price!

Grace Unlocked

A lovely pin of twisted gold,
Upon the dress, you wore so bold.
But as you danced, it took a leap,
Sailed through air, not very deep!

It landed down on Grandpa's pie,
He took a bite, oh my, oh my!
With jelly smeared all on his face,
He claimed it added style and grace!

"I'm now the king of fancy treats,"
He grinned while munching all the sweets.
While you just snickered at the scene,
A brooch was now a pie routine!

And as the laughter filled the hall,
You chose to wear it after all.
For grace unlocked with humor's key,
Brought joy to every pie-filled spree!

The Secret of the Jewel

A gem so bright, tucked in your hair,
You thought it chic, so full of flair.
But in the wind, it took a spin,
And knocked off twigs, a laughing din!

It whirled and twirled, away it flew,
Into the arms of a friendly shoe.
Your friend exclaimed, "What's this you've got?
A toe ring, maybe, quite a lot!"

You chuckled loud, a fashion mix,
A gem on feet, what a cool fix!
With every step, it jangled true,
The secret jewel that danced anew!

So next time you think of glamorous spark,
Just remember fun can leave a mark.
Wear laughter proudly, let it shine,
For fashion's most fun when it's divine!

Threads of Enchantment

In a world of glitter, the thread gets tight,
A squirrel is snooping, oh what a sight!
The pins are all dancing, the fabric takes flight,
While Grandma's still fussing, finding it right.

Needle and laughter, they braid and they weave,
As I trip on my hem, what a fun reprieve!
The fabric is grinning, it makes me believe,
That fashion has magic, if only you cleave.

Oh look at that pattern, it shimmies and shook,
A tailors' delight, oh come take a look!
With every small stitch, I'm caught in the hook,
Of chaos and giggles, like a fair fun book.

So let's thread the needle with tales of delight,
And create a fashion show, just for the night!
With bobbins and buttons, we'll start a fright,
Like glittering goblins, in sparkly light.

Essence of Radiance

A blink in the mirror, what do I see?
A smudge of lipstick, a rogue bumblebee.
Oh dear, what a mess, it's now part of me,
    This glamour parade is just too zany!

With sequins and ribbons, the cat makes a dash,
    While I try to balance my beauty stash.
The hairspray's a fountain, my lipstick's a splash,
    I'm ready for runway, let's make it a crash!

But wait, there's a snag in the sparkly dress,
The dog wants to join, oh what a big mess!
Now everyone gathers, I'm feeling the stress,
Yet laughter erupts, it's just pure happiness.

So I twirl and I whirl in this colorful scene,
A circus of charm, oh what could have been?
With joy as my armor and laughter my sheen,
    I strut on this stage—oh, beauty's routine!

The Jewel's Heart

A gem in the basket, it shines with glee,
It thinks it's a superstar, can't you see?
It wiggles and jigs, a true jubilee,
While I'm stuck wondering where's my cup of tea?

A sparkle here, a twinkle there,
The jewel tries to flirt, oh do take care!
For every sweet gleam, there's a tricky snare,
Like a cat and a yarn ball, it's so unfair!

With each little glimmer, it gains its own voice,
Singing sweet nonsense, oh what a choice!
But I just hold back, like it's my own noise,
Funny how beauty can be so poise!

So let's dance with the jewel, let's give it a spin,
A laughter-filled romp, let the chaos begin!
With sparkles and jokes, we'll surely win,
Embracing the madness, the fun lies within!

Celestial Beauty's Caress

The stars all gather, a cheeky affair,
To sprinkle their stardust in my wild hair.
With giggles and wonder, they light up the air,
Creating a ruckus, without a care.

But hold on, what's that? A comet in flight!
It zips through the room, a sheer delight.
I trip on my slippers, what a funny sight,
As beauty's allure turns chaos to light!

Planets are chuckling, they roll on the floor,
While Venus brings pizza, ask for some more!
Jupiter's winking, and oh, what a score,
These cosmic shenanigans leave us in awe!

So let's twirl and swirl under starlit embrace,
While beauty's mischief will quicken the pace.
With laughter and love in this vibrant space,
Together we shine, heart-to-heart, face-to-face!

Emblems of Radiance

In a drawer of treasures, hidden with flair,
A sparkle from nowhere, it caught my hair.
My cat wore it once, oh, what a sight!
Twirled like a ballerina, all day and night.

With glitters and gems, I tried to be bold,
But the pin gave a jab, oh how I scrolled!
It dances on jackets, a mischievous sprite,
A fashion faux pas that brought laughs at night.

The neighbors all gathered, their laughter did swell,
As I strutted my stuff, oh, they're under a spell!
But who's in charge here, me or the pin?
With every sharp poke, it makes me grin.

So button up, darlings, with pins that misbehave,
An emblem of radiance, a giggle to save.
For beauty may twinkle, and style may stick,
But laughter's the treasure that does the trick.

Whispers of Glamour

A whisper of glamour to wear on my sleeve,
I tried it on once, oh, how I did grieve!
It snagged on my sweater, what a surprise,
Did it wink at me? Just look at its eyes!

A gathering of friends with outfits so fine,
Yet my giggly sparkle, it turned into a vine.
Did I wear it too proud? Did I wear it too right?
It flung at my neighbors, a twinkling delight!

In the midst of the party, my brooch took a leap,
And landed on cake! What a mess, what a heap!
With frosting adorned, the laughter would bloom,
It's the star of the evening, consumed all the room.

In whispers of glamour, we toast with a cheer,
For fashion's a game, and laughter's the spear.
So let them all chatter about pins that we wear,
It's the joy in the laughter that truly laid bare.

Ethereal Trinkets

Ethereal trinkets, what fun do they bring?
They twinkle and jingle, like a joyful spring.
I pinned one on fluffy, oh, look at it bounce!
As if it were auditioning for a fashion pounce!

At the brunch with my pals, it sparked a debate,
Does that clip hold a secret, or is it just fate?
One thought it was vintage, an heirloom or more,
While I just adored it from the local store.

A fly landed once, did it think it could cling?
Caught unaware, suddenly I was king!
As I flailed wildly in my elegant chair,
The trinket just giggled, with flair in the air.

Ethereal trinkets, they shimmer and shine,
Yet tangled in mischief, they always align.
With each little laugh and every odd twist,
These gems of the funny do insist to persist.

Reflection of Style

A dazzling reflection, caught in a glance,
I sported my charm, thinking I'd dance.
But stuck to my coat, oh what a fuss!
Should I shimmy or shake? Oh, I wish it knew us!

The mirror chuckles with every new pose,
While my pin just sits there, like it's arose.
I tried a cool spin, but it twisted my fate,
Leaving me tangled, how could I sedate?

It gleams like the sun, but a nuisance it brings,
As friends start to giggle and point out my flings.
"Is that a new trend?" they ask with a wink,
Why yes, darlings, it's chaos, don't you think?

So let us embrace all the quirky the bright,
In reflections of style, laughter feels right.
For in each little awkward, we find the true glee,
That fashion, dear friends, is meant to be free!

www.ingramcontent.com/pod-product-compliance
Lightning Source LLC
Chambersburg PA
CBHW060143230426
43661CB00003B/554